WORKING WITH BUILDINGS AND STRUCTURES

KID ENGINEER

Izzi Howell

WAYLAND
www.waylandbooks.co.uk

First published in Great Britain in 2020 by Wayland

Copyright © Hodder and Stoughton, 2020

 Produced for Wayland by
White-Thomson Publishing Ltd
www.wtpub.co.uk

All rights reserved
ISBN: 978 1 5263 1296 9 (HB)
       978 1 5263 1297 6 (PB)

Credits
Editor: Izzi Howell
Illustrator: Diego Vaisberg
Designer: Clare Nicholas

Every attempt has been made to clear copyright. Should there be any inadvertent omission please apply to the publisher for rectification.

Printed in China

Wayland
An imprint of
Hachette Children's Group
Part of The Watts Publishing Group
Carmelite House
50 Victoria Embankment
London EC4Y 0DZ

An Hachette UK Company
www.hachette.co.uk
www.hachettechildrens.co.uk

The websites (URLs) included in this book were valid at the time of going to press. However, it is possible that contents or addresses may have changed since the publication of this book. No responsibility for any such changes can be accepted by either the author or the publisher.

All the materials required for the projects in this book are available online or from craft or hardware stores. Adult supervision should be provided when working on these projects.

CONTENTS

ENGINEERING BUILDINGS AND STRUCTURES

Engineers design and create things to solve problems. They work together with architects to design incredible buildings and structures, such as bridges and tunnels, which help us to get from one place to another.

First sketches

First, architects use their creative skills to design what the building or structure will look like. They draw sketches of their ideas. They might want the building or structure to stand out from or match other buildings in the area, for example.

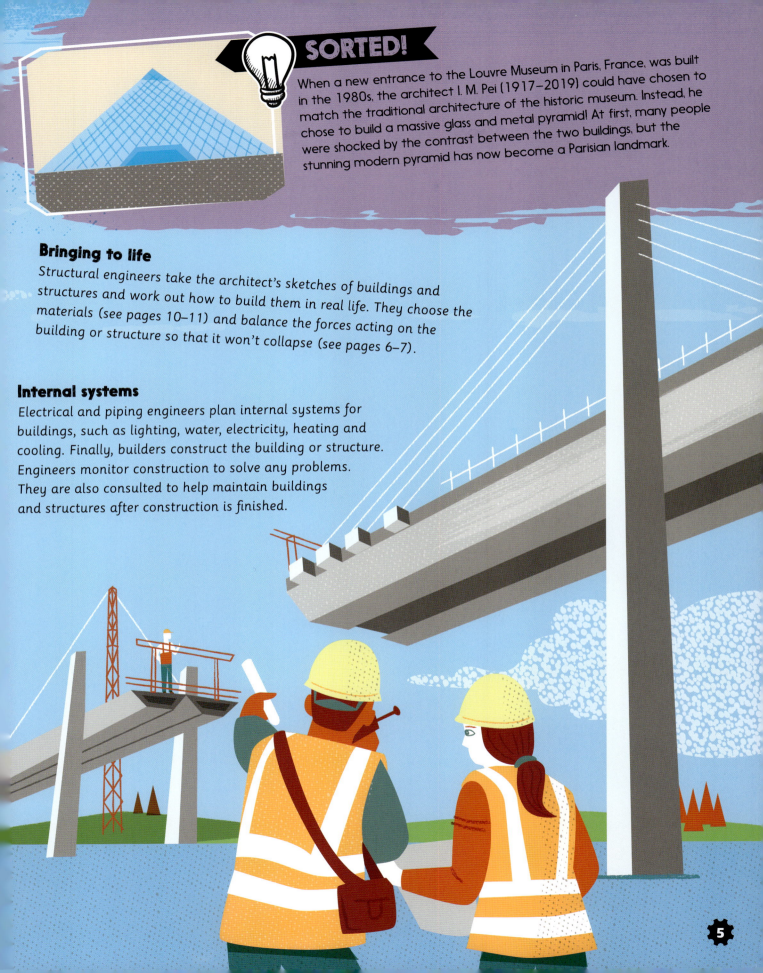

When a new entrance to the Louvre Museum in Paris, France, was built in the 1980s, the architect I. M. Pei (1917–2019) could have chosen to match the traditional architecture of the historic museum. Instead, he chose to build a massive glass and metal pyramid! At first, many people were shocked by the contrast between the two buildings, but the stunning modern pyramid has now become a Parisian landmark.

Bringing to life

Structural engineers take the architect's sketches of buildings and structures and work out how to build them in real life. They choose the materials (see pages 10–11) and balance the forces acting on the building or structure so that it won't collapse (see pages 6–7).

Internal systems

Electrical and piping engineers plan internal systems for buildings, such as lighting, water, electricity, heating and cooling. Finally, builders construct the building or structure. Engineers monitor construction to solve any problems. They are also consulted to help maintain buildings and structures after construction is finished.

FORCES AT PLAY

Many forces act on buildings, including gravity and the weight of the building itself. Engineers add features such as foundations and support beams to help balance these forces.

Sinking down

All of the materials in a building, such as bricks, glass and metal, plus people and furniture, add up to a considerable weight. Gravity also pulls the building down into the ground, resulting in a large downwards force. If engineers leave this force unbalanced, the building will sink into the ground. So, engineers add foundations that spread these forces across a wider area of the ground. This balances the forces and the building stays in place!

There are many different types of foundation. Some are better for use in certain soils, or for certain types of building or structure.

Falling over

Gravity can also make buildings and structures fall to one side. If an object's centre of gravity is not in the centre of its base, it can create a turning effect called a moment, which can pull a building over. Engineers also use foundations to solve this problem. The foundations push back against turning forces from wind, for example, and balance them, stopping the building from tipping over.

SORTED!

The Leaning Tower of Pisa, in Italy, is famous for its tilt. It started to lean during its construction in the twelfth century, because the ground it was built on wasn't strong enough to support its weight. By the late twentieth century, it was leaning around 5.5 degrees to one side. However, engineers have worked to stabilise the ground beneath the tower, and its lean is now only 4 degrees.

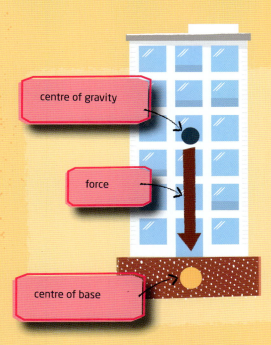

centre of gravity

force

centre of base

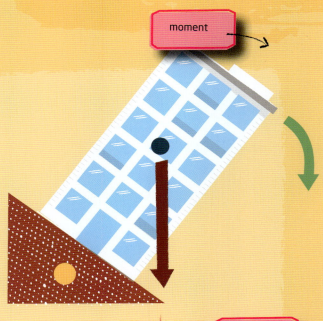

moment

weight

beam

Balancing weight

Buildings are usually hollow because space is needed for the rooms inside. To reduce the number of walls and pillars needed to support this hollow space, engineers use horizontal support beams in the floors. These beams also make the building stronger. Any weight placed on the floor is transferred sideways to the strong outer walls.

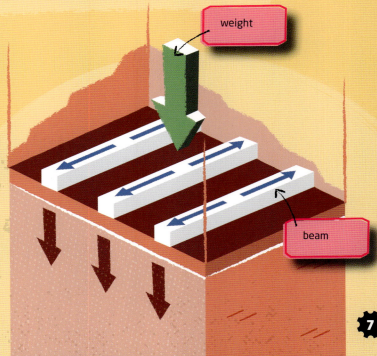

YOU'RE THE ENGINEER:
TAKE THE PAPER BUILDING CHALLENGE

You don't need traditional building materials to test the forces that affect buildings and structures. Experiment by making different structures from paper, and then take the paper building challenge.

You will need

Newspaper or scrap
　　paper
Scissors
Tape

Here are some structures you can make with paper:

Roll it tightly to make a narrow pillar.

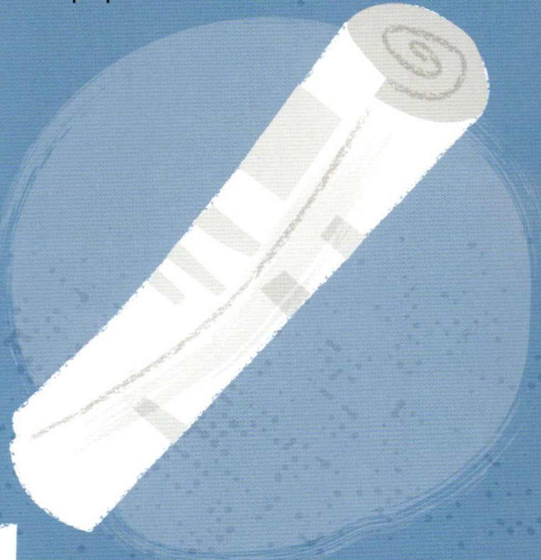

Roll and secure it with tape to make a wide column.

Cut slits to join two pieces together.

Fold it back and forth to make a fan shape.

Fold and secure it with tape to make a triangular or square piece.

Can you make the following structures from paper? You can use scissors to cut the paper and tape to hold the pieces together, but no other building materials. Use newspapers or scrap paper rather than wasting new paper.

- A structure that holds a book 15 cm off the ground
- The highest possible structure using just one A4 piece of paper
- A structure that holds an egg 30 cm off the ground
- A 30-cm-tall structure with no corners
- A pyramid or a building with a domed roof (see page 13)
- The biggest possible structure without using any tape
- A structure that sits on pillars
- A structure that you can fit inside.

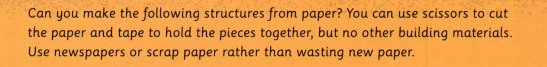

TEST IT!

Test different types and thicknesses of paper, such as standard A4 paper, thin card and newspaper. Which type of paper is best for each part of the building? Incorporate thick cardboard into your structures – can you make your buildings higher or stronger when you use cardboard as well as paper?

BUILDING MATERIALS

Engineers choose materials with different properties for each part of a building or structure. Some engineers are also developing new materials with special properties that will make building maintenance easier.

Strong structures

For the main structure of a building, engineers select materials that are strong, but not too heavy. They often combine materials to take advantage of their different properties. For example, reinforced concrete is made of steel bars inside concrete blocks. Concrete is cheap and easy to produce, while steel helps to make concrete stronger and more durable.

Decorative details

Because structural materials support the weight of the building, engineers can use decorative materials for the outside that aren't particularly strong, such as glass. However, exterior materials must be resistant to strong sunlight and rain. Engineers must also consider the cost and sustainability of all materials.

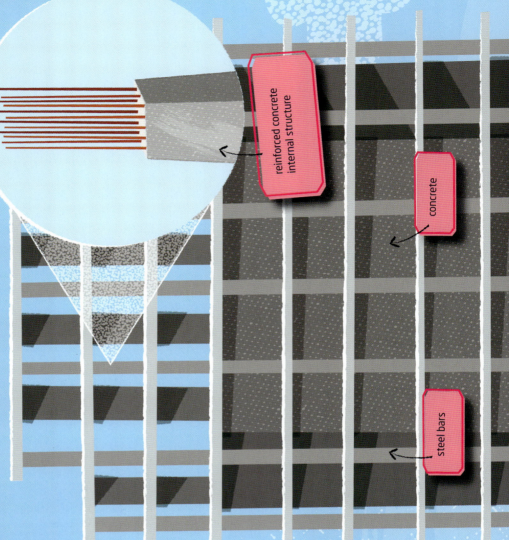

reinforced concrete internal structure

concrete

steel bars

Smart materials

Materials engineers are developing new smart materials for buildings that respond automatically to changes in their surroundings. For example, self-healing concrete can fix itself automatically if it cracks. The concrete contains pods of materials that turn into concrete when they come into contact with water, filling any gaps.

large glass panels

eco-brick

SORTED!

Engineers around the world, particularly in less economically developed countries, are embracing the eco-brick as a building material. The eco-brick is a plastic bottle that is packed full of flexible plastic waste until it becomes solid like a brick. It is an effective building material when combined with concrete and wooden rods. It is also cheap and helps to reduce waste.

ARCHES AND DOMES

Engineers often use arches and domes when designing buildings. As well as being attractive features, they are also excellent support structures that can bear a lot of weight.

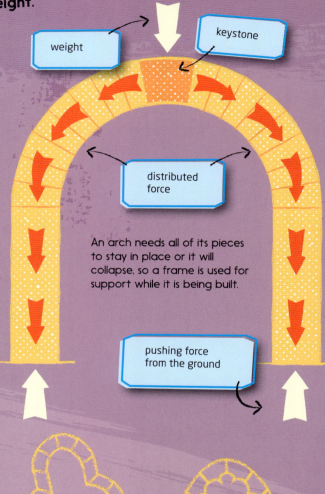

weight

keystone

distributed force

pushing force from the ground

An arch needs all of its pieces to stay in place or it will collapse, so a frame is used for support while it is being built.

Supporting itself

An arch supports its own weight, and the weight of its load, with compression (pushing) forces. The central stone, or keystone, bears the weight of the load. From the keystone, this force is pushed outwards into the other blocks that make up the arch. The weight travels into the ground or the supports beneath the arch, which push back and balance the force.

Roman arches

The Romans (6th century BCE to CE 4th century) were fantastic engineers, as we can see from the fact that many of their buildings have survived to this day! Roman engineers were some of the first to use arches in structures such as bridges, public buildings and aqueducts. They cut the pieces of the arch so accurately that they fit together perfectly.

SORTED!

Before domes were invented, pillars were used inside buildings to support the roof. These pillars took up a lot of space. The Romans realised that rotating an arch in a circle created a hollow half-sphere shape that could support its own weight, creating the first domed roofs!

Since the Romans, engineers have used domes as roofs and ceilings on countless buildings around the world.

US Capitol Building (Washington D.C., USA), designed by Dr William Thornton and others in the 18th and 19th centuries

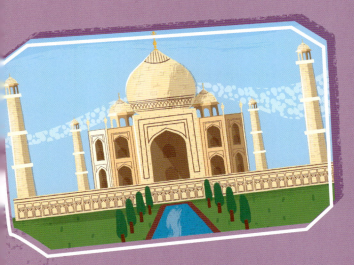

Taj Mahal (Agra, India), designed by Ustad Ahmad Lahori in the 17th century

St Basil's Cathedral (Moscow, Russia), designed by Posik and Barma (who may have been the same person!) in the 16th century

Dome of the Rock (Jerusalem, Israel), designed by Raja ibn Haywah and Yazid ibn Salam in the 7th century

YOU'RE THE ENGINEER:
MAKE A GEODESIC DOME

A geodesic dome is a dome made out of triangles, rather than arches. They are often seen in playgrounds. Try making your own geodesic dome from firm jelly sweets and toothpicks.

You will need
At least 11 firm jelly sweets
At least 25 toothpicks

1 Make a pentagon from five jelly sweets and five toothpicks.

2 Push two toothpicks into each jelly sweet, pointing upwards. Then, form triangles by attaching one jelly sweet between two toothpicks. This should form five triangles around the sides of the pentagon.

3 Join the top jelly sweets with five toothpicks to create another pentagon towards the top of the dome.

4 Stick one toothpick into each jelly sweet in the top pentagon. Then connect the toothpicks in the centre by poking them all into one jelly sweet. Your dome is complete! Press down gently on the top of it with your hand. How much weight can it resist?

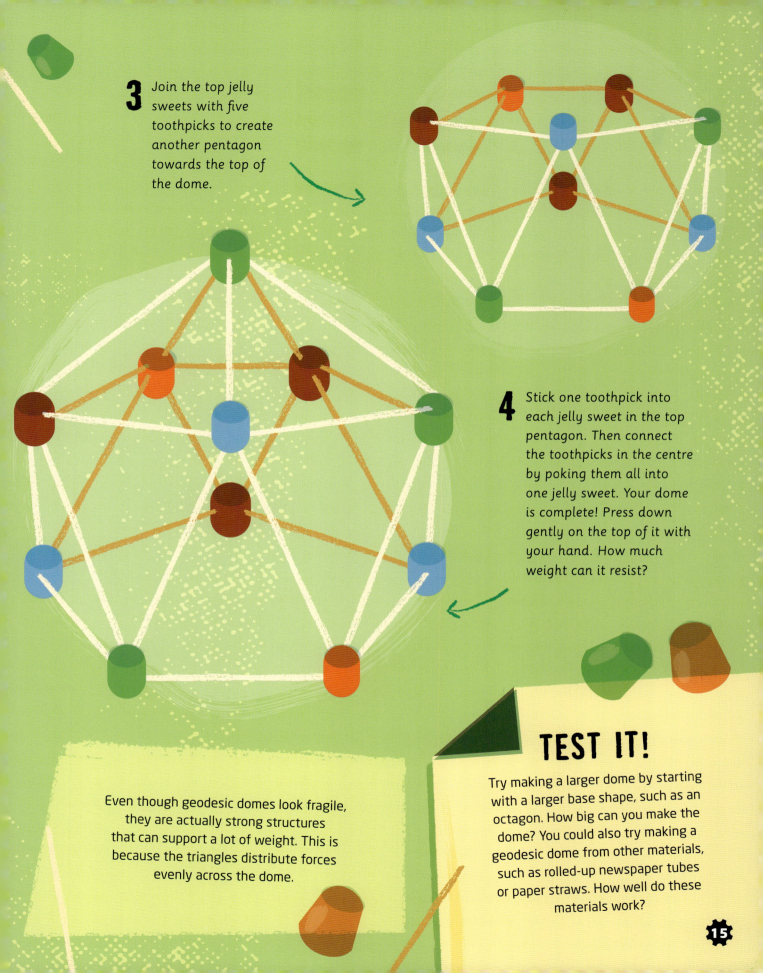

Even though geodesic domes look fragile, they are actually strong structures that can support a lot of weight. This is because the triangles distribute forces evenly across the dome.

TEST IT!

Try making a larger dome by starting with a larger base shape, such as an octagon. How big can you make the dome? You could also try making a geodesic dome from other materials, such as rolled-up newspaper tubes or paper straws. How well do these materials work?

SKYSCRAPERS

The first skyscrapers were built by engineers in the late nineteenth century. A new material, mass-produced steel, allowed them to build sky-high buildings for the first time in history.

Steel structures

The US engineer William Le Baron Jenney built the first skyscraper, the Home Insurance Company Building, in Chicago in the 1880s. He, and other engineers of the time, used steel as the internal structure of their skyscrapers. Steel is much lighter than other metals, so for the first time, engineers could build towering buildings that wouldn't collapse under their own weight.

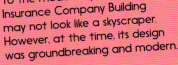

To the modern eye, the Home Insurance Company Building may not look like a skyscraper. However, at the time, its design was groundbreaking and modern.

Space in cities

The rise of the skyscraper was also linked to a need for more space. Many people in the USA moved to cities, such as Chicago and New York City, in the 19th century, and there wasn't enough space to build new homes and businesses for them all. Engineers found a solution by creating vertical space in skyscrapers. This was the beginning of the modern city, with skylines made up of tall buildings.

The world's tallest

Today, the race to create the tallest building continues. The Burj Khalifa in Dubai is currently the world's tallest building at 828 m. However, it may soon be overtaken as there is a building currently under construction in Jeddah, Saudi Arabia, that may reach 1 km in height. There are limits to the heights that skyscrapers can reach, but with new technology, materials and approaches, engineers will set new records.

SORTED!

Another invention was key to the development of the skyscraper – the lift! The US engineer Elisha Otis (1811–61) developed an early type of lift in the 1850s which was used in the first skyscrapers. Without a lift, it would have been very hard to get objects and people up to the higher floors.

The **Burj Khalifa** has one of the **fastest lifts** in the world. It takes just **one minute** to **travel** from the ground floor to the **124th floor**!

The tallest buildings in the world

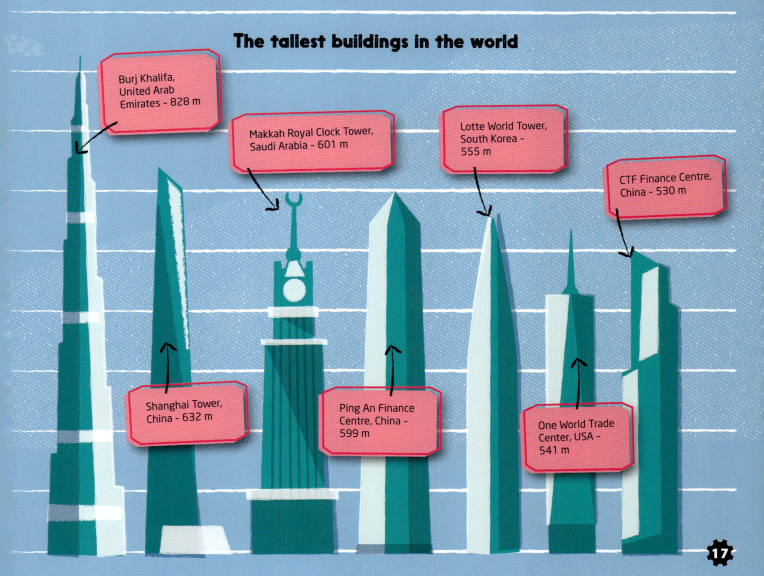

Burj Khalifa, United Arab Emirates – 828 m

Makkah Royal Clock Tower, Saudi Arabia – 601 m

Lotte World Tower, South Korea – 555 m

CTF Finance Centre, China – 530 m

Shanghai Tower, China – 632 m

Ping An Finance Centre, China – 599 m

One World Trade Center, USA – 541 m

BRIDGES

Bridges allow us to travel across spaces that would otherwise be hard to cross, such as rivers. Bridges require careful engineering and design. If the forces acting on a bridge are unbalanced, the bridge can bend and collapse.

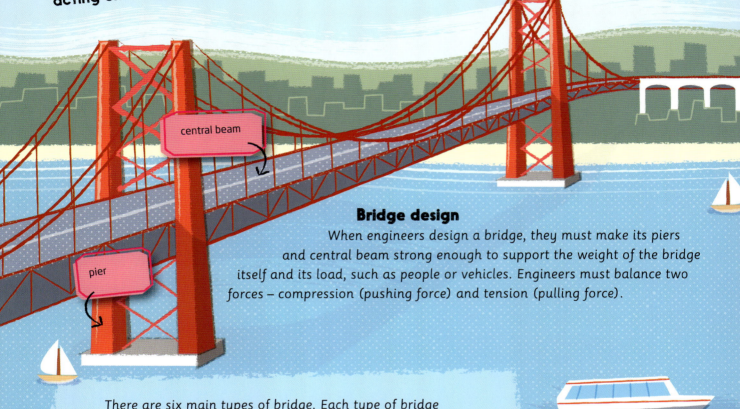

central beam

pier

Bridge design

When engineers design a bridge, they must make its piers and central beam strong enough to support the weight of the bridge itself and its load, such as people or vehicles. Engineers must balance two forces – compression (pushing force) and tension (pulling force).

There are six main types of bridge. Each type of bridge balances compression and tension forces in different ways.

Arch

Like the arches used in buildings (see pages 12–13), arch bridges support weight through compression. They need to have very strong, solid foundations, as this is where the weight of the bridge and its load is supported.

Beam

The first bridges were simple beam bridges, such as a tree trunk laid across a stream. Today, beam bridges still have the same design, with a flat beam and two or more piers. Engineers tend to use beam bridges for short distances, as a long beam bridge would require too many piers.

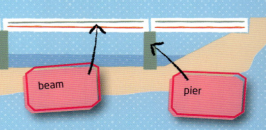

beam

pier

Cantilever

Cantilever bridges are made of two sections that are only secured at one end. The bridge is anchored to the land at each side, with a central beam resting on the unsupported ends of the two sections.

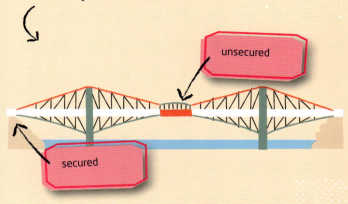

unsecured

secured

Cable-stayed

In a cable-stayed bridge, the beam is suspended with long cables from one or more tall towers. Engineers design these bridges so that most of bridge's load is transferred into the towers along the cables. The load then passes from the towers into the ground.

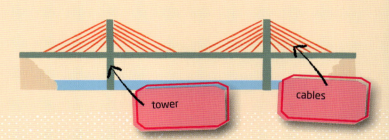

tower

cables

Suspension

In a suspension bridge, the beam is suspended from both curved and straight cables. Engineers use suspension bridges to span very long distances.

Truss

A truss bridge has a basic metal structure similar to a beam bridge. However, the truss provides additional support as the load is spread out over a wider area. This means that the bridge can resist more force.

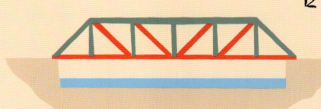

The **oldest bridge** in the **world** that is still in use is a **stone arch bridge** in Turkey, which dates back to **850 BCE!** Bridges did exist before then, but they have **fallen apart** or **rotted away.**

Choosing a design

Engineers choose a type of bridge depending on its location. For example, if a bridge is needed to cross a long distance, engineers would probably use a suspension or cantilever design instead of a beam bridge, because these bridges are stronger over longer distances. For a short, simple bridge across a road, they might choose a simple beam or arch rather than a more complex bridge.

YOU'RE THE ENGINEER: BUILD BRIDGE MODELS

Build and test bridge models made from card. Discover how they work in different spaces and how they can be made stronger.

You will need

7 cm x 12 cm index cards
Books
Tape
Two toy cars or small
plastic figures
A pencil

Beam bridge

Start by making a beam bridge. Make two piles of books of the same height and place one index card spanning the distance between them to create a bridge. Place your car on the bridge. What happens to the bridge? Could it support two cars?

Arch bridge

Next, test an arch bridge by bending another card into an arch and placing it in the space underneath the beam bridge. You may need to adjust the height of the book piles so that it fits. Test the arch bridge with the car. What happens? How does the arch bridge compare to the beam bridge?

Cantilever bridge

Now, test a cantilever bridge. First, make piers for your bridge. Take a card and fold it into thirds. Fold it into a triangle shape and secure with tape. Repeat three more times so that you have four piers.

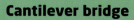

Tape two index cards together along their short sides to make a longer beam and place it across the two piles of books. Tape each end down to the books. Place two piers under the middle section of each card (you may need to adjust the height of the books). Test with the cars and compare its strength to the other bridges.

TEST IT!

Can you make any other types of bridge using these materials, such as a cable-stayed bridge? Use other materials to improve your bridges or make another type of bridge, such as a truss bridge from lolly sticks.

TUNNELS

Tunnels are very useful, allowing people to easily move across barriers such as mountains, rivers and busy city roads. However, excavating a tunnel is a complex engineering challenge.

Planning ahead

First, engineers have to choose the best location for the tunnel. They survey the area, checking the type of soil or rock and looking for underground water, cables, other tunnels and any other obstacles. Planning ahead in this way helps to avoid delays later on.

Risk of collapse

As with the engineering of all buildings and structures, designing tunnels is about balancing forces. The lining of the tunnel must be able to resist the force of the surrounding soil or rock pushing inwards. Engineers use strong materials such as stone, concrete, steel or iron to line the inside of tunnels for this reason.

pushing force from surrounding soil or rock on tunnel

pushing force from tunnel lining on surrounding soil or rock

Cutting tunnels

Engineers use a a tunnel boring machine (TBM) to cut tunnels through rock. After the rock has been cut away, the TBM supports the new tunnel until the lining is installed. Otherwise, the tunnel would collapse immediately. Once the lining has been installed, hydraulic jacks push the TBM forwards and it continues to excavate the tunnel.

A tunnel boring machine has a circular plate at one end that rotates and slices into the rock.

Removed rock is carried to the other end of the TBM on a conveyor belt.

The **Delaware Aqueduct** is the **longest tunnel** in the world. It carries water from the **Delaware River** over **137 km** to **New York City!**

The British engineer Sir Marc Isambard Brunel (1769–1849) is well-known for the construction of the Thames Tunnel in London, England. This was the first tunnel ever built under a river. The secret to Brunel's success was a tunnel shield that he invented. The shield held the tunnel in place while tunnel workers built the lining. Brunel was the father of engineer Isambard Kingdom Brunel (1806–59), who designed bridges, railways and steamships.

MOVING AND SHAKING

Engineers design buildings and structures to resist extreme conditions, such as strong winds or earthquakes. This helps to keep people safe and reduce damage during these violent events.

Earthquake danger

During an earthquake, shockwaves travel through the ground, creating horizontal push and pull forces. These waves can make a building collapse. This is very dangerous for people inside the building and nearby.

Flexible foundations

One way in which engineers make buildings more earthquake-resistant is by placing a layer of springs or flexible posts between a building and its foundations. This allows the foundations to move separately with the shockwaves, so that the building isn't pulled over.

Flexible exterior steel frames bend with the shockwaves and hold the building together.

Flexible posts in the foundations allow the building to move with the ground, rather than against it.

Engineers have also developed other strategies to make buildings safer during earthquakes.

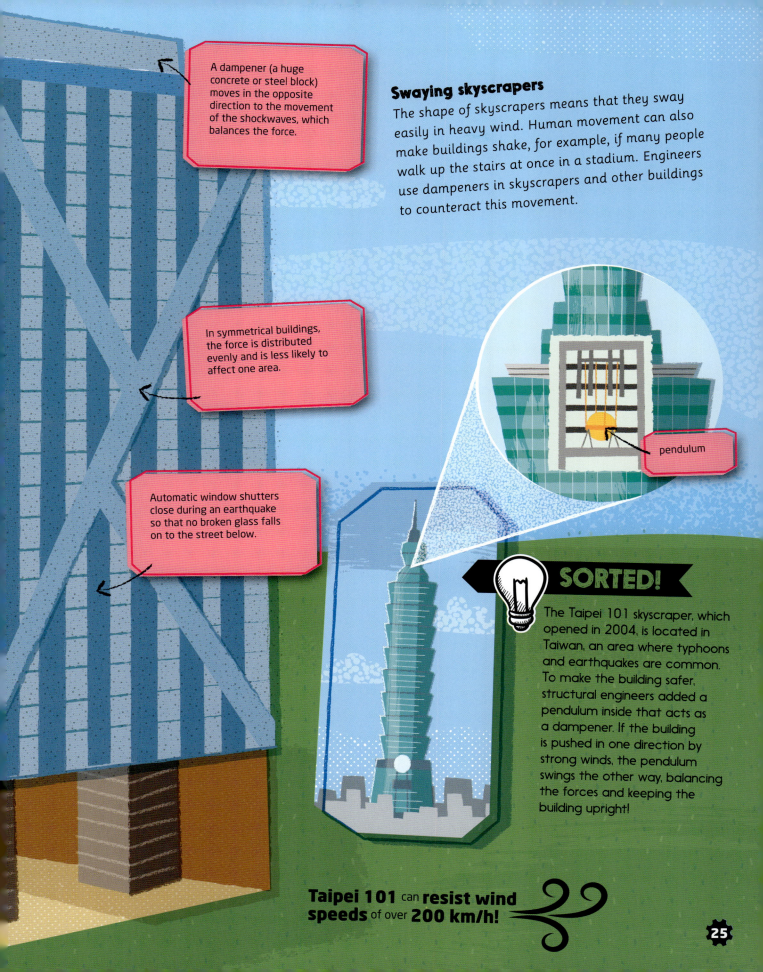

A dampener (a huge concrete or steel block) moves in the opposite direction to the movement of the shockwaves, which balances the force.

In symmetrical buildings, the force is distributed evenly and is less likely to affect one area.

Automatic window shutters close during an earthquake so that no broken glass falls on to the street below.

Swaying skyscrapers

The shape of skyscrapers means that they sway easily in heavy wind. Human movement can also make buildings shake, for example, if many people walk up the stairs at once in a stadium. Engineers use dampeners in skyscrapers and other buildings to counteract this movement.

pendulum

SORTED!

The Taipei 101 skyscraper, which opened in 2004, is located in Taiwan, an area where typhoons and earthquakes are common. To make the building safer, structural engineers added a pendulum inside that acts as a dampener. If the building is pushed in one direction by strong winds, the pendulum swings the other way, balancing the forces and keeping the building upright!

Taipei 101 can **resist wind speeds** of over **200 km/h!**

YOU'RE THE ENGINEER: TEST BUILDINGS IN JELLY

Use jelly to create the conditions of an earthquake and put a model building to the test. Are your engineering skills succesful enough to keep your building upright, or will it fall over in the wobbly jelly?

You will need

A deep metal or glass tray
1 or 2 packets of jelly
Mini marshmallows
Wooden toothpicks or
    dry spaghetti

1 Prepare the jelly the night before you want to do your experiment. Follow the instructions on the jelly packet to make up one or two packets of jelly, depending on the size of your tray. Ask an adult to help you boil the kettle to prepare the jelly.

2 By the next morning, the jelly should have set in the tray. Now, prepare your structure. Use the marshmallows and toothpicks or pieces of dry spaghetti to assemble a simple tower. Begin by making squares and triangles and then join them together to make 3D shapes, such as pyramids, cubes and cuboids. Your tower must be at least two toothpicks high.

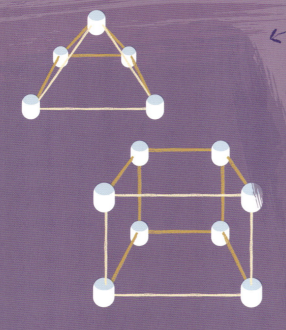

3 Place your tower in the tray of jelly. Tap the sides of the tray or shake it gently to create waves in the jelly, similar to earthquake shockwaves. What happens to your tower? Does it sway with the waves or fall over entirely?

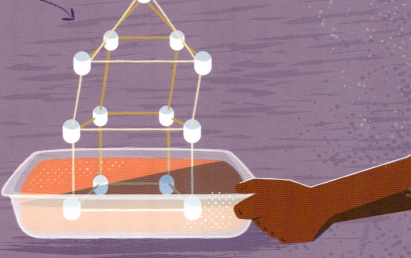

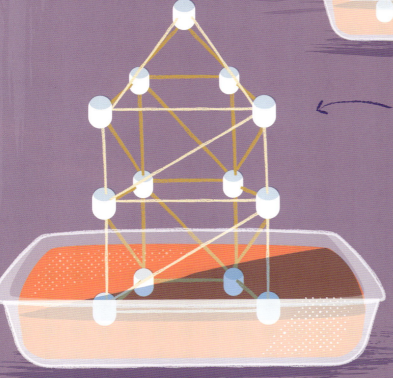

4 After testing your tower, rebuild it so that it is more resistant to the shockwaves. You could add diagonal beams to make the walls stronger or the base bigger. Use your knowledge of the techniques that engineers use in real buildings to make your tower stronger. For example, how could you add foundations?

5 Keep testing your tower and improving it until you have built the ultimate earthquake-proof building!

TEST IT!

Try using other materials, such as cardboard, to add to your tower or create a new tower. How resistant are they? Challenge yourself to create the tallest tower that won't fall over. How tall can you make it?

AMAZING BUILDINGS AND STRUCTURES

Engineers combine creative skills with their advanced knowledge of forces and materials to create some of the most incredible structures in the world.

Spiky station

The architect Santiago Calatrava (1951–) and his engineering team are responsible for the stunning Oculus structure, located above the World Trade Center Transportation Hub in New York. The Oculus is made up of two rows of long steel spikes with windows in between. The windows let light into the station below. A central truss distributes the weight of the spikes evenly across the building.

The Oculus is supposed to look like a bird being released from a child's hands. This is a tribute to the people who lost their lives when the original building on this site was destroyed in the 9/11 terrorist attacks.

During construction, the spikes were added one by one to the central truss.

Complex curves

The Heydar Aliyev Center in Baku, Azerbaijan, is well-known for its unusual folded, curved shape. It was designed by Zaha Hadid and her team of engineers, who achieved this shape by using a lightweight metal lattice as the structure for the building. The lattice was flexible enough to be folded, but still strong enough to support the building. The centre contains an auditorium, galleries and a museum.

Zaha Hadid (1950–2016) was a British-Iraqi architect known for her striking, modern buildings. Many of her designs had bold, curved shapes, as seen on the Heydar Aliyev Center. She used technology to engineer these complex designs before they were brought to life.

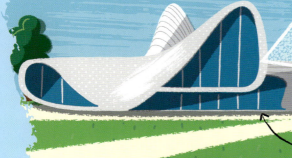

The outside of the Heydar Aliyev Center is covered in very thin pieces of concrete reinforced with glass. The pieces are laid in a way that makes it look like one giant piece covers the whole building.

Geodesic roof

The AAMI Park stadium in Melbourne, Australia, has a distinctive roof made up of geodesic domes. The domed roof is self-supporting, which means that all the spectators can see the pitch, with no pillars in the way. The building was designed by a team of engineers at Cox Architecture, and is mainly used for football and rugby matches.

The outside of the AAMI Park stadium is covered with thousands of LED lights. The lights can be programmed to display different images and patterns.

The **geodesic roof** structure of the **AAMI Park stadium** required **50 per cent less steel** than a standard stadium roof.

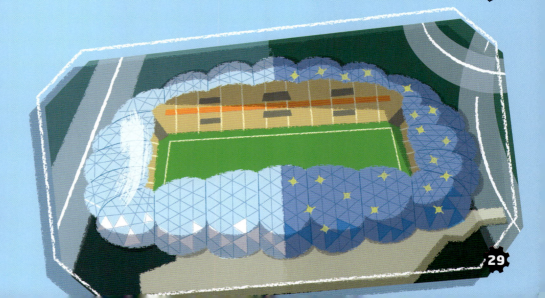

GLOSSARY

architect someone who designs new buildings and checks they are built correctly

aqueduct a structure for carrying water across land

balanced when two or more forces are the same strength

compression a pushing force

excavate to dig a hole in the ground

foundations the underground structures that support a building

gravity a force that pulls things towards each other

horizontal parallel to the ground

hydraulic jack a machine that uses liquids to provide power to lift other objects

lattice a structure made from strips that cross over each other with spaces in between

pendulum a weight on a stick or thread that moves from side to side

pier a column used to support a bridge

property a quality of a material, such as hard, soft or flexible

reinforced concrete concrete with steel bars inside it for strength

resistant not easily changed or damaged

skyscraper a tall building with many floors

stabilise to make something stronger and unlikely to change in the future

sustainable causing little or no damage to the environment and able to continue for a long time

symmetrical describes something that looks the same on both sides

tension a pulling force

typhoon a violent tropical storm

unbalanced when one force is greater than other forces, which results in a change to the motion of an object

vertical standing upright

FURTHER INFORMATION

Books

Buildings (Adventures in STEAM) by Izzi Howell (Wayland, 2017)
EcoSTEAM: The Houses we Build by Georgia Amson-Bradshaw (Wayland, 2018)
Engineering (Building the World) by Paul Mason (Wayland, 2019)

Websites

www.pbs.org/wgbh/buildingbig/lab/forces.html
Test how forces affect bridges.

easyscienceforkids.com/all-about-tunnels/
Learn more about tunnels.

www.youtube.com/watch?v=iGRLY08Kn2o
Watch a video of a civil engineer explaining how to build strong foundations.

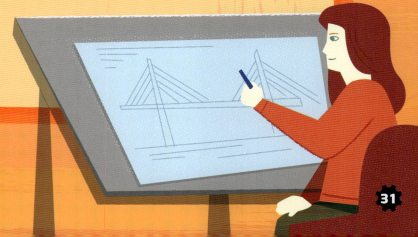

INDEX